Reading Wo
Discovery W

LEVEL 6

Lost in the forest

Catherine Adenle

Series Editor – Jean Conteh

MACMILLAN

About this Book

To the Teacher
or Parent

This story, which should interest both boys and girls, is set in a real place – Mole National Park in Ghana. The author, Catherine Adenle, comes from West Africa, and loves the wild animals that live there.

The book has seven chapters, and two information sections at the end.

On pages 48–49, there are maps to show where Mole National Park is. On pages 50–53, there are pictures of some of the animals that live there.

Use the book like this:

- Before the children begin the book, check that they know where Ghana is.

- Ask the children which animals they have seen, and where they saw them.

- Let the children try to read the book by themselves, encouraging them to work out the meanings of any new words.

- When the children have finished the story, ask them if they enjoyed it. Let them discuss it with other children.

- On pages 54–55, there are some questions and activities that are designed to help the children enjoy the story more and understand it better.

Above all, let the children enjoy reading this book. Then they will want to read more books for themselves, and so become independent readers.

Chapter 1

I'm bored!

Ednah was twelve years old. She lived with her parents in Accra, the capital city of Ghana.

She was a very lucky girl. Accra is a beautiful city, and Ednah's parents loved her and took good care of her. She went to a good school, and lived in a lovely house.

There was only one problem. It was the school holidays, and Ednah was bored.

She sat in her father's rocking chair on the veranda of her parents' lovely house in Accra, and yawned.

'I'm bored!' she said, as she looked up to the sky. She had played every video game in the house and watched her favourite shows on television. She closed her eyes for a second and was soon fast asleep.

A little while later, a strange man's voice woke her.

He was calling from the other side of the road.

'Is this Mrs Kandie's house?' he shouted.

'Yes, it is,' Ednah replied.

'I've brought this letter for her from the village,' said the man.

'Thank you,' Ednah shouted. She ran across the road to get the letter. Then she went inside the house to give it to her mother.

'Mum, this is a letter for you from the village,' she called.

Ednah was impatient to know what was in the letter.

'What's in the letter, Mum?' she kept asking, as her mother read the letter.

Before Ednah could ask her question for the tenth time, her mother said, 'It is from Grandpa and Grandma. They want us to go to the village because we haven't visited them for a long time.'

Ednah was very excited. At last, she would no longer be bored.

'We are going to the village, we are going to the village,' she sang, while she danced around the house.

She decided to go and tell her friend, Roselyn.

'I am going to the village on Tuesday, to see my grandparents,' she said to Roselyn.

'What is there for you to do or see in the village?' asked Roselyn. She thought the village would be boring, compared with Accra.

'I don't know,' replied Ednah. 'I might see some animals. Mum told me that people come from all over the world to see the animals near the village.'

The village was near Mole National Park, the biggest game park in Ghana. The journey there would take two days.

Ednah and her mother would have to leave very early in the morning. They would go by bus, first to Kumasi, then to Tamale, a big city in the north of Ghana. They would spend the night there.

The next day, they would take another bus to the village.

'Don't forget to take your camera. Bring back some pictures for me to see,' said Roselyn.

'What a good idea. Perhaps the village won't be so boring, after all,' Ednah thought.

On Monday, Ednah was packing her bag for the trip to the village, when her mother walked into her room.

'You won't need those video tapes in the village,' her mother laughed.

'Why not?' asked Ednah.

'There's no electricity there!' replied her mother.

'Does that mean there's no television?' Ednah asked, sadly.

Her mother nodded.

'I'm afraid so.'

'But what am I going to do in the village?' asked Ednah. 'I'm going to be so bored.'

'Don't worry. There's plenty for you to see and do. Don't forget, I grew up there. I had as much fun at your age as you do now, even without television,' smiled her mother.

The next day, Ednah woke up very early. She stood in the bathroom and looked in the mirror.

She made faces and then started to dance and sing, 'I am going to the village, I am going to the village!'

Her mother heard her singing and shouted, 'If you're coming with me to the village, you'd better be ready on time!'

Ednah went on dancing.

'Hurry up!' called Ednah's mother. 'We're leaving soon.'

'Yes, Mum!' said Ednah.

Afraid that her mother would leave without her, she had her bath quickly, put on her clothes and brushed her teeth.

Ednah's father had to stay in Accra, to work. He took Ednah and her mother in his car to the motor park in the centre of the city. That was where they caught the bus.

'Have a great time in the village!' he shouted to them, as he waved 'goodbye'.

The old bus drove through the city before setting off on the road north, to Tamale. It was a long way. The smooth tarmac road gradually became rough and bumpy.

'This bus is so uncomfortable. I wish Dad could've driven us to the village,' Ednah whispered to her mother.

She wondered if they would ever arrive.

Chapter 2
Amina

When they finally arrived at the village, everybody gave Ednah and her mother a warm welcome. Grandma and Grandpa were very happy to see Ednah. They hadn't seen her since the last time they came to Accra. That was four years ago.

But Ednah was not so happy to find out that her home for the next two weeks was an old mud house with a thatched roof. There was no running water and no electricity.

Ednah looked around at every inch of the small house. Her mother was right. There really was no television.

'I'm going to be so bored,' she moaned.

She went to the back of the house to the place where her grandfather kept his animals.

She saw a herd of cattle with iron bells hanging around their necks. She also saw some chickens and their chicks.

'Oh, these baby chicks are so cute!' she cried. She picked one up. One of the hens clucked very loudly, shook its feathers and began to chase her.

'Help! Help! A chicken is after me!' Ednah shouted, at the top of her voice.

She ran so fast that she thought she had beaten the Olympic record for a hundred metres.

'Ednah, put the chick down!' shouted Grandma.

Ednah dropped the chick, and the mother hen stopped chasing her.

Breathing heavily, Ednah said, 'Thanks, Grandma. That was very scary!'

'Mother hens protect their young very fiercely, you know. Let that be a lesson to you,' explained Grandma.

After all the excitement of being chased by the hen, Ednah went back inside the house.

She started complaining to her mother again, 'Mum, there are no beds here.'

'Don't worry, there are mats behind the doors,' replied her mother.

'Mats? You mean we are…' began Ednah, but before she could say another word, her mother called out to a girl sitting in front of the house across the road.

'Amina, Amina! Come and meet Ednah!' she called.

Amina came towards Ednah's mother and smiled.

'Hello,' she said quietly.

Ednah thought Amina looked beautiful in her beaded jewellery and her red wrap-around cloth.

'Hello,' Ednah replied.

Amina was very happy to meet a city girl. She had never been to the city.

The girls quickly became friends. Amina showed her new friend everything in the village. They climbed trees to pick fruit together.

Amina loved Ednah's clothes and her sunglasses with their city style. She tried one of Ednah's dresses and the sunglasses. She walked around, shaking her waist.

'How do I look?' she asked, laughing.

'You look beautiful,' Ednah replied politely, although secretly she thought that Amina looked a bit like a waddling penguin.

Then Ednah took her camera out of her bag.

'What's that?' asked Amina.

'It's a camera,' replied Ednah. She held it up so Amina could see. Then, she said, 'I'm going to take your picture. Say cheese!'

She pressed the button to take Amina's picture. Amina thought the light from the flash was very bright. She was still blinking as Ednah gave her the camera so she could see it more closely.

After her initial shyness, Amina was as talkative as a parrot. She talked about everything to Ednah.

'Papa told me that I can go and work as a vet in the city when I grow up. I love animals, I want to look after them.'

'What does your father do?' asked Ednah.

'He is a tracker for the people who are protecting the animals in the park.'

'What's a tracker?' Ednah asked, curiously.

'A tracker knows how to recognise the footprints of animals, and follows them,' replied Amina.

'You mean, his job is following wild animals?' asked Ednah.

'Yes,' replied Amina, 'and he has shown me how to recognise different animals by their footprints, and also how to find your way in the bush so that you don't get lost.'

'Sometimes, my father even flies in a helicopter with Mr Benson to check on the animals roaming the forest in the park,' she went on. 'They have to see if the animals are all right.'

'Wow! I would like to fly in a helicopter. It must be fun,' said Ednah. Then she asked, 'Who is Mr Benson?'

'He's from Accra. He's a wildlife expert. He told the villagers that living animals are worth more money to them than dead ones,' said Amina.

'I'd like to take some photos of wild animals to show my friends back home,' said Ednah.

'I'll take you to see some animals tomorrow,' promised Amina. 'We'll go for a walk in the forest to see them.'

Chapter 3

Into the forest

Next morning, Ednah woke up to the sound of a cock's crow.

Her mother shouted, 'Ednah, get up if you want to go with Amina to fetch some firewood! She's waiting in front of the house.'

'Yes, Mum,' answered Ednah.

She got up and went to the front of the house.

'Let's go!' said Amina.

'Wait! Let me get ready and find my camera,' said Ednah, and she rushed inside.

On the way to the forest, they saw people herding their cattle. Ednah asked, 'Are we going to see some wild animals now?'

'No, not yet,' replied Amina. 'We might see a few. We have to walk a long way into the park to see the animals. They'll be on the plains and the grasslands, looking for food.'

Ednah was impatient.

'I really want to take pictures of animals. Please take me to see them!' she begged. 'You did promise.'

'Yes. OK. I'll take you to see the animals as soon as we've collected the firewood. My mum needs it to cook,' replied Amina.

'Thanks!' Ednah gave her friend a hug.

The two girls collected up two bundles of firewood as quickly as they could. They took it back to the village for Amina's mother. Then they set off together, to walk deep into the forest.

Ednah had never seen such interesting sights.

'What's that?' she asked, pointing at a brightly-coloured shape.

Amina picked up a glowing green animal. Ednah looked at it cautiously. She watched the animal as it suddenly changed colour.

'It's a chameleon!' answered Amina. 'Take its picture,' she urged.

Amina placed the chameleon carefully back on the tree branch. It then changed colour again.

'What an amazing animal!' said Ednah.

'Yes, they do that to blend in with their surroundings, so that nothing can see them,' replied Amina.

'How did you know that?' asked Ednah, as she took its photograph.

'Papa told me. He used to be the best hunter in the village. I went hunting with him once and he taught me all about the animals of the forest,' replied Amina.

They walked a little further, then suddenly Amina said, 'Look! That's a dung beetle!'

She pointed to the beetle on the forest floor. Ednah stared at it.

'Watch. It's rolling the dung on the floor into balls. Then it will bury it as food for its young. Hurry, take a picture,' said Amina.

They walked further and came out of the forest and into the open plain.

'Look!' said Amina again. 'That's a pangolin ripping apart the termite mound.'

Ednah looked on with interest.

'Sh-h-h-h…' whispered Amina. 'Watch. It uses its long, sticky tongue to suck up the termites from the holes in the mound.'

Ednah stood and watched quietly. She looked curiously at the hard, leaf-shaped scales that covered the pangolin's small body.

'Did you know that pangolins have no teeth?' asked Amina.

'Really?' Ednah said, sounding surprised.

'Watch this! It's going to roll up into a ball and play dead when I touch it,' Amina said.

She poked the pangolin gently, with a stick. Both girls laughed as the pangolin curled up like a ball.

'I am enjoying this walk!' smiled Ednah.

The long walk got more and more interesting.

After a while, Ednah began to get tired.

She said to Amina, 'I'm tired. I need to take a rest.'

Amina found some bananas growing nearby, and the girls sat down under a shady tree and began to eat one each.

Suddenly, they heard noises above them. They looked up and saw that monkeys were swinging from branch to branch of a nearby tree, and squirrels were running up and down the tree-trunks. An excited monkey jumped up and down.

'Look at those monkeys!' whispered Ednah.

'Don't be afraid. Take some more pictures,' whispered Amina in reply. Ednah's hands were shaking as she took the pictures. Then she felt something like water on her arms.

'Has it started raining?' asked Amina.

The girls looked up. A cheeky monkey was urinating on them! The girls both laughed and quickly ran away from the trees.

Suddenly, Amina shouted, 'Careful! Watch out!' Ednah looked down. A snake wriggled and wove its way through the grass in front of them on the forest floor.

Ednah was frightened. She jumped up and put her hand over her wide open mouth to stop herself from screaming.

'I could have stepped on that,' she gasped. 'Oh, that was close. I hate snakes!'

'I once captured a snake that crawled into our house. I put it in a basket for my parents to see when they came back from the farm,' said Amina proudly.

'That was a dangerous thing to do,' said Ednah.

'I know,' replied Amina. 'Papa was very angry with me, because the snake might have had poisonous venom in its teeth. But Mama thought I was a very brave girl.'

Chapter 4

Are we lost?

By now, the girls were very hot, thirsty and hungry. They found a large mango tree. Juicy mangoes were hanging from its branches.

They were big and ripe, and just waiting to be picked. The girls could not believe their luck as they sank their teeth in to them. They sucked the sugary juice out of the fruit and closed their eyes as they enjoyed the sweetness of the mangoes.

Licking her lips, Ednah said, 'This is most delicious! I'll take some more for later.' She picked two more mangoes and the two girls sat under the tree, enjoying the rest in the cool shade. Suddenly, the leaves and shrubs near them started to move. Something was coming.

'Stay calm. Most animals are not dangerous unless they are in danger. Just ignore them, as if they are not here,' said Amina.

Ednah was terrified.

'What should we do now?' she whispered.

Some baboons came out of the leaves. A young one touched Amina's face.

'The baboon's hands look just like human hands. The only difference is that they belong to a baboon,' Ednah thought to herself. The young baboon touched Amina's lips and ears. It also touched Ednah's camera.

Ednah was so afraid that she closed her eyes, but quickly opened them again. She saw Amina reach up and stroke the baboon's back gently. She was amazed.

Then a naughty baboon came and took the mangoes she was holding, and ate them! Amina began laughing.

The girls continued their walk towards a lake.

'That's a hippo!' exclaimed Amina. A large, plump animal splashed about in the waterhole by the lake. Its eyes, ears and nose were above the water.

'Let me take its picture,' Ednah said, quietly.

'Look over there, near the shrubs. Do you see the crocodile enjoying an afternoon snooze by the river bank?' Amina said.

'Where?' Ednah asked.

'There!' replied Amina.

The crocodile slowly swung its head around and blinked sleepily. Ednah saw another crocodile. She thought she saw it smile a toothy grin, showing off its fearsome set of sharp teeth.

'The crocodiles are waiting for animals to come and drink in the waterhole. They hide in the water and swim slowly to their prey. They then grab it and drag it under water to eat. Papa said they are hunted for their skins. People use them to make leather goods,' explained Amina.

The girls crept through the bushes and long grass. They saw an animal, grunting its way through the bushes, alone.

'That must be the most ugly animal in the whole park. What is it?' whispered Ednah.

Laughing out loud, Amina replied, 'It's a warthog – a wild pig.'

Then she pointed above her head.

'Look at that beautiful bird!' shouted Amina as a long-legged stork flew above their heads.

Then Ednah saw some strange-looking birds.

'What are those?' she asked, pointing up at them.

'They are vultures, looking for dead animals to feed on,' explained Amina.

Suddenly, there was a loud R-O-A-R!

Frightened, Ednah looked at Amina and said, 'Did you hear that?'

'What?' asked Amina.

'That mighty roar,' said Ednah. 'Are there lions here?'

She was trembling.

'Maybe. Papa told me that he once heard a lion roaring,' replied Amina.

'Let's go now. I've seen enough animals,' said Ednah, anxiously.

'No, let's see some more,' replied Amina.

But Ednah was really frightened now.

She shouted, 'I'm going back to the village!'

She clutched her camera and started to run.

Amina ran after her.

'Yes, you're right. There must be lions and leopards about because they feed on these animals. We must get out of here!' she shouted. 'Papa told me they always wander around the waterholes. Let's run!'

Ednah took her sandals off and ran even faster. She was really scared – and even Amina looked a bit afraid.

Soon, they were back among the trees.

It was getting dark in the forest. The girls went on running but, in their confusion, they did not look where they were going.

'Is this the way? asked Ednah.

'I don't know,' replied Amina. She looked around.
'Oh no! I think we're lost.'
    Ednah said, 'I thought you knew the way!'
    She began to cry.

Amina felt worried now too, but she also felt angry with Ednah. There was no need to cry! But secretly, she wanted to cry, too.

'We're a long way away from the village,' said Amina quietly.

Ednah looked at her friend in disbelief. 'Are we really lost?' she asked.

'Yes, I think we are,' said Amina.

Chapter 5

Where are we?

Tired and weak, the girls came to a clearing and sat down.

After a while, they could hear footsteps.

'There are people,' Ednah thought. 'Maybe we'll be rescued!'

She opened her mouth to say something, but Amina touched her arm.

'S-h-h-h-h… Don't make a sound,' she whispered. 'Quiet. They could be poachers.'

'What are poachers?' Ednah whispered back.

'They kill animals illegally to sell them,' replied Amina. 'They kill them for their body parts, like their fur, or their horns, or tusks.'

Then, they heard the footsteps of the two men even nearer, and their shadows made the dark forest even darker.

The girls kept as still as they could, until the poachers passed. They both felt very frightened now.

Amina knew that she had to keep calm. She had to find the way home. Ednah did not know what to do.

'Listen,' Amina said to Ednah. 'I know it's very scary now that it's beginning to get dark. But we must try to find our way. If we don't get back to the village by nightfall, everyone will be very worried about us.'

She put her arm round Ednah's shoulder. Amina could feel that her friend was shaking. She knew she had to hide her own fear. With their arms round each other for warmth, the girls sat in the clearing and thought about what to do.

Amina was right. Back in the village, the girls' families were getting worried.

Amina's father went out on the track for a short distance with some other men, to see if the girls were on their way, but they could see nothing. He knew that it would very difficult to find them in the dark.

Ednah's mother felt very frightened, but she tried to be brave as she waited for the searchers to return. When the men came back without Amina and Ednah, she felt like crying. They tried to comfort her.

'Don't worry,' said Amina's father. 'I'll go to Mr Benson's house now, and ask him if we can search with the helicopter. Then we'll soon find them.'

He soon returned with a promise from Mr Benson
that they could use the helicopter. But they would have
to wait until morning. It was being used for other work,
and it was not possible to get it back before then.

'The only thing left,' said Amina's father, 'is to take
the jeep as far as we can along the track. Let's hope we
see them.'

'I'm coming with you,' said Ednah's mother.

Chapter 6

Finding the way

Amina crouched down to the ground. It was still light enough to see the grass and soil, and she studied it closely.

She went a short distance into the forest, then returned. Ednah watched her. She was not crying now, but she still felt very frightened.

'I think the baboons came this way,' Amina said. 'I can just see a few footprints and some places where the grass has been pulled. Let's go this way. I'll look out for more tracks.'

Holding hands, and in silence, the two girls made their way into the forest. Amina looked very, very carefully all around her.

It was getting almost too dark to see tracks on the ground, but she was also looking for signs of the baboons on the grass and on the trees.

Meanwhile, Amina's father was driving the jeep very slowly along the track towards the forest. Everyone was looking out of the windows, as carefully as they could, to see if there was any sign of the girls.

The jeep stopped every now and then, and everyone got out and walked away from the track a few yards on either side to see if they could see anything. In this way, they went slowly through the forest.

In the forest, Amina and Ednah edged forward, very slowly now, as it was getting quite dark. Amina was finding it very difficult to see the tracks of the baboons.

She was beginning to get worried about Ednah, who would not let go of her hand. The noises of animals moving through the forest, or calling to each other, were really making them afraid. Amina could feel her friend's body shaking. She thought Ednah might faint.

Just then, Amina noticed the shape of a tree not far ahead of them. She remembered it from earlier in the day. She could also just see that its branches were covered with fruit. She almost laughed with relief.

'Look, Ednah,' she said gently. 'That's the mango tree where we met the baboons today. They have brought us back to it. We're safe!'

At the same time, the jeep was travelling slowly through the forest. It was quite dark now, and its headlights shone into the trees ahead of them.

Suddenly, Amina's father noticed something moving along the track ahead.

'There they are!' he shouted, and pointed at the two small figures that could just be seen in the headlights.

As the jeep approached, the figures stood quite still. Amina's red wrapper glowed in the strong light.

'Thank God you're safe!' shouted Ednah's mother, as she stumbled out of the jeep and rushed to embrace her daughter and her friend.

Chapter 7

Back to the city

The next morning, the whole village knew the story, and many people came to see Ednah and her mother. Everyone was very happy to see that Ednah and Amina were safe. The girls apologised to their parents for making them worried.

'I… I… I'm sorry, Mum. I promise never to go anywhere again without telling you,' said Ednah in a quiet voice.

Her mother gave her a hug.

'Is it really so boring in the village?' she asked.

Ednah smiled. 'No, Mum. And even though it was scary, I had fun taking pictures of animals in the forest. I took lots of pictures. I can't wait to show Dad and my friends back home.'

'Twelve-year-old girls shouldn't wander too far into the forest. It's too dangerous,' said Amina's father.

'Papa, I'm sorry for wandering into the forest, and because I didn't look after Ednah,' said Amina.

'Well,' said Amina's father, 'I'm happy that you found your way. That shows that you have learned about animal tracks. Now, Mr Benson has just been on the radio. He's happy that you're both safe. He's coming in the helicopter soon. We are going to search for a sick elephant. Someone saw it limping on the grassland yesterday. He asked if you and Ednah would like to come with us.'

Amina and Ednah were very excited. They had never been in a helicopter. Ednah ran to find her camera.

Soon, they saw the helicopter in the sky above them.

It flew over the village, then landed on some level ground nearby. Everyone ran to see the helicopter. The girls climbed in, along with Amina's father. Amina closed her eyes and held on to her father as the helicopter took off. Ednah looked down at her mother and grandparents in the crowd of villagers who were watching the helicopter. Its four giant blades rotated fast as it flew off over the forest.

The girls smiled as they looked down and saw how small the trees and animals below looked.

'Everything is so small from up here,' Amina said, still holding on to her father. The girls could see all the places where they had walked the day before – the track, the forest, the lake, even the clearing where they looked for the way home.

'Look! Look!' Ednah shouted and pointed to the clearing.

There, just near the big mango tree, were their friends, the baboons.

The next morning, Amina and Ednah had to say 'goodbye'.

Ednah sat on the bus, which was just about to leave. Amina stood outside. Ednah put her hand out of the window of the old bus.

'Bye! I'll miss you,' she cried, as she wiped tears from her eyes.

'Bye-bye,' Amina waved back to Ednah.

Tears were rolling down her cheeks, too. As the bus drove away, she waved until she could see it no more.

Back at home, Ednah showed her pictures to Roselyn.

'All the animals are really beautiful. Well, except for the ugly warthog,' laughed Roselyn.

Ednah looked at all her pictures again. 'I'm glad I went to the village. I had a lot of fun! I met a new friend and had a ride in a helicopter.'

'That's certainly better than watching television,' said Roselyn, with envy.

'Wait until I show the pictures to my teacher and my friends at school. I'll tell them all the things Amina told me about each animal,' said Ednah proudly. She closed her eyes for a minute and stretched.

'Ah-h-aha, I'm bored here,' she yawned.

Both girls laughed.

Mole National Park

Mole National Park is a big wildlife park in the north of Ghana. It was made into a park in 1957. You can see many different West African wild animals there. Here are some maps. One shows you where Ghana is, and where the park is. The other map shows the journey that Ednah and her mother made from Accra to Mole National Park.

Mole National Park

GHANA

Map of Africa

BURKINA FASO

BENIN

GHANA

Mole National Park

Tamale

TOGO

IVORY COAST

Bus route

Kumasi

Accra

Gulf of Guinea

Animal tracks

Ednah and Amina found their way home safely because Amina knew how to recognise animal tracks and other signs in the forest.

Leopard

We can learn a lot about wild animals and their habits from their tracks. This can help us to find our way in the forest or the bush, like Amina and Ednah. Expert trackers, like Amina's father, can also use what they learn from animal tracks to protect wild animals from poachers, like the ones the girls saw in the story.

If you could visit Mole National Park in Ghana, you would see many different animals. There are pictures of some of them here and on pages 52–53. Look at their feet. What sort of tracks do you think they might make?

Warthog

Honey badger

Olive baboons

Colobus monkey

Chameleon

Activity Page

1 What differences did Ednah notice between Accra and the village? Read Chapter 2 again, and make a list of them. See if you can find more than five differences.

2 Do you live in a city or a village? Which do you think is best? Choose one of these places and write some sentences about why you think it is the best place to live. Begin your sentences like this: 'I think it is good to live in a village because...' or 'I think it is good to live in a city because...'

3 In Chapter 3, we read that Ednah was very 'impatient'. What was she impatient about? Can you find any other places in the story where she was impatient? Write a short character sketch of Ednah.

4 Make a list of all the animals and birds that Ednah and Amina saw in the forest and by the lake. Find out as much as you can about them. Write a description of your favourite animal and draw a picture of it.

5 Why were the girls quiet when they saw the poachers (in Chapter 5)? Why do you think people poach animals? Can you suggest some of the ways in which poachers can be stopped?

6   Imagine that you are Ednah. Write a letter to Amina, two
     weeks after you return to Accra from the village. What
     would you write about? Tell Amina about life in Accra.
     You could talk about school, your friends and so on.